A Small Book of Essays on Peacemaking Criminology

A Small Book
of Essays
on Peacemaking
Criminology

Louis J. Gesualdi

HAMILTON BOOKS

Lanham • Boulder • New York • London

Published by Hamilton Books
An imprint of The Rowman & Littlefield Publishing Group, Inc.
4501 Forbes Boulevard, Suite 200, Lanham, Maryland 20706
www.rowman.com

86-90 Paul Street, London EC2A 4NE

British Library Cataloguing in Publication Information Available

Library of Congress Cataloging-in-Publication Data

ISBN: 978-0-7618-7454-6 (pbk : alk. paper)
ISBN: 978-0-7618-7455-3 (ebook)

♾ ™ The paper used in this publication meets the minimum requirements of American National Standard for Information Sciences—Permanence of Paper for Printed Library Materials, ANSI/NISO Z39.48-1992.

This book is dedicated to my friend and colleague Professor Thomas Ward.

Contents

Preface

A peacemaking approach to criminology is a humanistic perspective to criminology. It is a humane, nonviolent and scientific approach in its treatment of crime and the offender. A peacemaking approach to criminology deals with prevention of crime and rehabilitation of offenders, and involves principles of social justice and human rights. The collection of writings chosen for this book demonstrates a peacemaking approach to criminology.

Chapters 1 presents the case for a different way about dealing with crime known as a peacemaking approach to criminology (which includes restorative justice).

In chapter 2, the beliefs of the Muscogee community are listed and these beliefs are a major part of the roots of peacemaking criminology.

Chapter 3 presents the successful work of John Augustus in probation that exemplifies the principles of peacemaking criminology.

In chapters 4, needs of the U.S. healthcare system are examined from a peacemaking point of view.

Chapter 5 indicates that a peacemaking approach to criminology not only supports the implementation of different intermediate sanctions but also of changes in the social and economic structures of American society.

In chapter 6, it is shown that the commonly held beliefs about Italian Americans and organized crime are inaccurate.

Chapter 7 analyzes the harmful acts committed by the well-off.

In chapter 8, it is made known that capitalism as is, tends to undervalue many things, activities and people which are core to the human experience.

Chapter 9 lists the social characteristics that favor the development of creative genius in a society.

Chapter 10 presents the initial stages of a plan for a development of economic democracy.

In chapter 11, a list of many of the things that Leonardo da Vinci did during his lifetime is provided and this list may help us as individuals become the best creative person we can be.

Chapter 12 provides a list of questions and problems that future research by peacemaking criminologists need to answer.

It is this author's wish that these 12 chapters will stimulate a desire by the reader to become interested in peacemaking criminology.

Acknowledgements

I make the following acknowledgements. Chapter three, "The Work of John Augustus: Peacemaking Criminology," was originally published by the Academy of Criminal Justice Science as "The Work of John Augustus: Peacemaking Criminology" in the newsletter *Academy of Criminal Justice Science ACJS Today*, Volume XVII, Issue 3, September/October, 1999, Louis Gesualdi, the author. Chapter five, "Peacemaking Acts and Programs to Cut Adult and Teen Crime," was originally published by the Pennsylvania Sociological Society as "Peacemaking Acts and Programs to Cut Adult and Teen Crime" in the journal *Sociological Viewpoints,* Vol. 19, 2003, Louis Gesualdi, the author. Second, I wish to thank Dr. Luca Landoli, Dean of the Lesley H. and William L. Collins College of Professional Studies of St. John's University, for his support and assistance that enabled me to write this book.

Introduction

A peacemaking perspective to criminology, according to H. Pepinsky and R. Quinney[1], is a humanistic approach to criminology. This approach views crime as just one of the many forms of suffering (such as war, poverty, unemployment and others) that characterize human existence. It is involved with the advancement of humane, non-violent, non-authoritarian and scientific ways to reduce (and eventually end) suffering and oppression. A peacemaking viewpoint proposes major changes of the social and economic structures in the United States (as well as the rest of the world) so that these structures no longer bring about suffering and oppression.[2]

Chapter one, "A Peacemaking Perspective to Criminology," points out that a peacemaking approach "emphasizes social justice, conflict resolution, rehabilitation and a belief that people need to cooperate in democratic institutions in order to develop meaningful communities."[3] This approach in its treatment of crime and the offender looks both at a person's responsibility and at the contribution of society's organizations.[4] Peacemaking criminology is a humane, nonviolent and scientific way to effectively cut crime in America.[5] This chapter provides a brief discussion on peacemaking criminology.

The second chapter, "The Muscogee Community: Peacemaking Criminology," lists the beliefs of the Muscogee Community, a Native American group located in the state of Oklahoma. These listed beliefs demonstrate the peace and love that are so highly valued among the Muscogee group. The tenets of peace and love exemplify and are the roots of Peacemaking criminology.

Chapter three, "The Work of John Augustus: Peacemaking Criminology" demonstrates that John Augustus' work in probation was quite successful and exemplified the principles of peacemaking criminology (involves not an authoritarian but a humane, nonviolent and scientific approach in its treatment of crime and the offender). This chapter argues that the implementation of alternative sanctions and a full employment bill is a continuation and expansion of John Augustus' successful work and would be supported by peacemaking criminologists.

The fourth chapter, "The Future of Healthcare in the United States" lists the main components, according to Peacemaking Criminology, that are needed in a future model of the U.S. Healthcare System. It also lists, from a peacemaking view, the workforce challenges that will need to be dealt with by the U.S. Healthcare System in the future.

Chapter five, "Peacemaking Acts and Programs to Cut Adult and Teen Crime," indicates that a peacemaking approach to criminology not only supports the implementation of different intermediate sanctions but also of changes in the social and economic structures of American society. These changes include a full employment bill, a real minimum wage, universal health care and ending the prohibition of drugs. This chapter asserts that such political acts and programs would provide adult and teen offenders rehabilitation and a real chance to better their lives.

The sixth chapter, "Popularly Held Beliefs about Organized Crime: A Peacemaking Critique," demonstrates that the commonly held beliefs about Italian Americans and organized crime are inaccurate. This chapter also reports social scientific studies indicating that Italian Americans did not develop organized crime in the United States. In other words, this chapter represents a peacemaking view of crime and criminology by its examination of the misinformation on crime and criminal justice (stigmas held about Italian Americans and organized crime) and by its presentation of a more accurate picture of criminal behavior (data presented that shows a more accurate depiction of Italian Americans).

Chapter seven, "A Peacemaking Approach Dealing with the Criminal Elite," examines the harmful acts committed by the well-off (criminal elite). Such acts include embezzlement, bribery, computer crimes, crimes against the consumer (fraud, unsafe products), medical crimes, and environmental crimes (pollution, unsafe workplaces). In its analysis of these harmful acts, peacemaking criminology points out the bias against the poor that exist within America's criminal justice system.[6]

The eighth chapter, "Human Capitalism," makes known that peacemaking criminology agrees with Andrew Yang's that capitalism as is, tends to undervalue many things, activities and people which are core to the human experience. Also, this chapter indicates that peacemaking criminology, in agreement with Yang's book, supports the development of Human Capitalism.

Chapter nine, "Social Characteristics that Favor the Development of Creative Genius: A Peacemaking View," in its brief discussion of Silvanno Arieti's socio-historical book *Creativity: The Magic Synthesis*, lists the social characteristics that favor the development of creative genius in a society. This chapter maintains that a peacemaking view of criminology, as a movement, supports the development of such a society.

The tenth chapter, "A Development of Economic Democracy," is the beginning of a blueprint for a development of economic democracy. This chapter contends that an economic democratic system may eliminate or significantly lower the amount of social problems associated with the market economy (such as unemployment, underemployment, poverty, unsafe work conditions and destruction of the environment).

Chapter eleven, "Lessons Learned from Leonardo to Help Develop More Creative Individuals," in its examination of Walter Issacson's book *Leonardo Da Vinci,* provides a list of many of the things that Leonardo da Vinci did during his lifetime and this list may help us as individuals become the best creative person we can be. Peacemaking criminology encourages individuals to learn the lessons from Leonardo da Vinci for their own creative personal development and using this creativity to help develop a more creative society.

The twelfth chapter, "Future Peacemaking Research" provides a list of questions and problems that future research by peacemaking criminologists need to answer.

The twelve chapters of this book are a beginning to an understanding of peacemaking criminology. It is the author's wish that this publication will stimulate a desire by the reader to become more interested in this humane approach to criminology.

NOTES

1. Harold Pepinsky and Richard Quinney, eds., *Criminology as Peacemaking* (Bloomington: Indiana University Press, 1991).

2. Ibid.

3. John R. Fuller, *Criminal Justice: A Peacemaking Perspective* (Boston: Allyn and Bacon, 1998), 41.

4. Ibid, 43.

5. Fuller, *Criminal Justice: A Peacemaking Perspective.*

6. Jeffrey Reiman and Paul Leighton. *The Rich Get Richer and the Poor Get Prison: Ideology, Class and Criminal Justice,* New York, NY: Routledge, 2023.

1

A Peacemaking Approach to Criminology

A peacemaking perspective to criminology, according to H. Pepinsky and R. Quinney[1], is a humanistic approach to criminology. This approach views crime as just one of the many forms of suffering (such as war, poverty, unemployment and others) that characterize human existence. It is involved with the advancement of humane, non violent, non authoritarian and scientific ways to reduce (and eventually end) suffering and oppression. A peacemaking viewpoint proposes major changes of the social and economic structures in the United States (as well as the rest of the world) so that these structures no longer bring about suffering and oppression.[2] This chapter provides a brief discussion on peacemaking criminology.

A peacemaking approach "emphasizes social justice, conflict resolution, rehabilitation and a belief that people need to cooperate in democratic institutions in order to develop meaningful communities."[3] This approach in its treatment of crime and the offender looks both at a person's responsibility and at the contribution of society's organizations.[4] Peacemaking criminology is a humane, nonviolent and scientific way to effectively cut crime in America.[5] Through the scientific way, a peacemaking approach points out the misinformation about issues dealing with crime and criminal justice and presents a more accurate image of such issues.

Peacemaking Criminology supports drug decriminalization. It declares that American society needs to view drug use as of a public health problem than a criminal justice issue and suggests that there are benefits from drug decriminalization. First, a peacemaking position explains that repealing drug laws will save billions of dollars a year in law enforcement. Second, this position makes apparent that organized crime would experience a severe setback as an outcome of drug decriminalization. Third, peacemaking criminology contends that the quality of life for many drug users would improve greatly if legal controls were removed.[6] For instance, many drug users may seek help without the fear of being arrested.

A peacemaking viewpoint to criminal justice rejects capital punishment on the grounds of social justice. This viewpoint notes that factors such as social status and race "make it more likely that some will be executed while others who are equally guilty will be spared."[7] Moreover, it makes evident that capital punishment is not an effective deterrent to murder.[8]

The accessibility of firearms, as argued by peacemaking criminology, is an important factor influencing the high rate of lethal violence in America. Peacemaking criminology explains that "other countries have a much lower rate of lethal violence that can be attributed to the lack of availability of guns."[9] It also contends that more gun control laws need to be developed and enforced in order to reduce such violence in our nation.

A peacemaking perspective to violence states that "poverty of our knowledge about violence and its prevention is considerable."[10] This perspective advances the following suggestions. First, more funding is needed for "programs and research efforts that might be able to identify and prevent violent behavior."[11] Second, myths and stereotypes about violent offenders and their victims need to be exposed. Third, methodological issues in data collection and analysis of violent offenders need to be improved. Fourth, more rehabilitative programs need to be set up for violent offenders.[12]

Research points out that a peacemaking perspective to criminal justice is highly successful in its treatment of crime and the offender. A peacemaking perspective, in the use of humane, nonviolent and scientific ways to effectively deal with unethical behavior, can balance the needs of victims, communities, and offenders.[13]

A peacemaking viewpoint draws from a variety of ancient wisdom and religious traditions including Judaism, Christianity, Islam, Hinduism, Buddhism, Taoism and Native American. In other words, the peacemaking perspective supports and promotes the tenets of peace and love (found in all religious traditions) in dealing with unethical behavior (for instance, peaceful movements for change by Gandhi and Martin Luther King). Also, a peacemaking approach draws from feminist traditions of equal rights, equal opportunities and cooperation and from critical traditions of social justice, enlightenment and freedom.[14]

Peacemaking criminology is directly relevant to corrections. It is against capital punishment and the construction of super maximum-security prisons. It points out that capital punishment and super maximum-security prisons work against the reduction of violence in society. Moreover, peacemaking criminology sees rehabilitation programs for offenders as a way to protect society.[15]

Restorative justice programs (such as victim-offender reconciliation programs, family group conferencing and victim offender panels) exemplify a peacemaking viewpoint. These programs, allow victims and offenders to meet one another outside the courtroom to hold offenders culpable for their misdeeds and to have offenders make reparation to their victims. A peacemaking viewpoint maintains that restorative justice programs can be of benefit to both victim and offender and that the criminal justice system in the United States is in need of these programs.[16]

Peacemaking criminology can be highly successful in dealing with unethical and criminal behavior. An individual can develop a peacemaking approach to criminal justice and society and become a force for personal and social peace[17] (see chapter "The Work of John Augustus: Peacemaking Criminology" as an example).

NOTES

1. Harold Pepinsky and Richard Quinney, eds., *Criminology as Peacemaking* (Bloomington: Indiana University Press, 1991).
2. Ibid.
3. John R. Fuller, *Criminal Justice: A Peacemaking Perspective* (Boston: Allyn and Bacon, 1998), 41.
4. Ibid, 43.
5. Fuller, *Criminal Justice: A Peacemaking Perspective.*
6. Ibid.
7. Ibid, 231.
8. Ibid.
9. Ibid, 197.

10. Ibid, 170.

11. Ibid, 179.

12. Fuller, *Criminal Justice: A Peacemaking Perspective.*

13. Michael Braswell, John Fuller, and Bo Lozoff, *Corrections, Peacemaking and Restorative Justice: Transforming Individuals and Institutions* (Cincinnati, OH: Anderson Publishing Company, 2001).

14. Ibid.

15. Ibid.

16. Ibid.

17. Ibid.

2

Muscogee Community

The Muscogee (Creek Nation) is a Native American group located in the state of Oklahoma.[1] This group, originally situated in Alabama, Georgia, Florida and South Carolina, has an ongoing, documented history in the United States going back before 1500 AD.[2] Listed below are the tenets or beliefs of the Muscogee.

- The importance of respect for all human beings.
- The absence of hierarchical, forced authority with the objective of consensus in decision making.
- Individual freedom coupled with the person's awareness of responsibility to the whole group.
- The importance of extended family with the additional respect for both the children and the seniors.
- The undertaking of systems of justice that center on the health-giving of society and the restoration of sense of balance, rather than retribution or vengeance.[3]

The above listed beliefs demonstrate the peace and love that are so highly valued among the Muscogee group. Furthermore, the tenets of peace and love exemplify and are the roots of Peacemaking criminology.

NOTES

1. Muscogeenation.com

2. See Glenn T. Morris. "For the Next Seven Generations: Indigenous Americans and Communalism." *Communities Directory*. Langley, Washington: Fellowship for Intentional Community.1995 and see fivecivilizedtribes.org.

3. See Morris, "For the Next Seven Generations: Indigenous Americans and Communalism" 1995.

3

The Work of John Augustus
Peacemaking Criminology

The United States has one of the largest and most costly prison systems in the world, as it incarcerates more of its population than most nations.[1] In response to this state of affairs peacemaking criminology has developed as a branch of criminology to champion alternatives to incarceration. Peacemaking criminology involves not an authoritarian but a humane, nonviolent and scientific approach in its treatment of crime and the offender.[2] It looks at crime as just one of the many types of suffering that illustrate human existence. Efforts to prevent such suffering, according to peacemaking criminologists, should include a major reconstruction of America's social institutions, such as the economic system and the criminal justice system, so that they no longer produce suffering.[3] Unemployment and incarceration are, respectively, aspects of America's economic system and criminal justice system that need alterations. In brief, the U. S., as a society pays no heed to prevention but rather follows the belief of imprisonment and punishment. Peacemaking criminology seeks prevention and rehabilitation to pursue the principles of social justice and human rights.[4]

The precepts of peacemaking criminology can be traced back to John Augustus who in 1841 introduced probation to the criminal justice system in the United States. His development of probation, like peacemaking criminology, was based on a humane, non authoritarian, and a scientific approach to deal with the offender. Augustus' view was that the "object of the law is to reform criminals, and to prevent crime and not to punish maliciously, or from a spirit of revenge."[5]

From 1841 to 1858, John Augustus had bailed out from jail 1150 males and 794 females. Of the two thousand people he bailed, only 10 proved ungrateful or absconded. In addition to those he bailed, he had helped over three thousand females who were destitute. Overall, he worked with offenders categorized as drunkards, extremely poor, unemployed, prostitutes and for the benefit of juveniles.[6]

Augustus performed many duties for the people who were placed on probation under his care. He made sure the person attended school or engaged in honest employment. He often arranged living accommodations and maintained records of all the cases he handled. In some cases, Augustus had some of his clients living in his own home. This sometimes involved rehabilitation of the offender with a drinking problem or providing shelter for women and children who were poor, unemployed and had no place to go.[7]

John Augustus insisted that the offenders who were drunkards had to "take the pledge" or promise not to drink liquor. Over 80% of the drunkards that he worked with became temperate and orderly citizens and gained employment. He showed that drunkards on probation under his care had greater success of rehabilitation than the punitive methods of jail or house corrections. For instance, he noted that the largest numbers of people in jail in the county of Suffolk in 1841-42 were drunkards. Augustus indicated that almost all the drunkards "were sentenced more than once, some as many as fifteen or twenty times" and that frequently only a few days would pass between the release and return of offenders to jail as a result of continued drunkenness. Augustus showed conclusively that imprisonment as a punitive measure, and in the extreme, "had a very slight tendency to produce the reformation of those who are its subjects."[8] In other words, jail or extreme punishment in general does not reform drunkards, that is, individuals with a substance abuse problem.

John Augustus' work representing peacemaking criminology in action had helped reduce crime without incarceration. His labors, as stated previously, were humane and non-authoritarian (that is, providing a home, working to rehab the drunkard, helping to gain employment for the person) and scientific (that is, keeping records of observations and applying methods that were found to be successful). Furthermore, similar to peacemaking criminology, he promoted alternative sanctions rather than prison in dealing with certain offenders.

Augustus' work can provide a basis for the development and further growth of peacemaking criminology. In examining American prisons, there are similarities with the kinds of people who are incarcerated today and the kinds of individuals John Augustus was able to rehabilitate outside of prison.

There is a telltale pattern to the person incarcerated today in the United States. Thirty-five percent were unemployed at the time of their arrest and most of those who had been working had very low paying jobs. Drug offenders represent the largest proportionate growth of inmates, increasing from an estimated 58,000 in 1983 to 354,000 in 1993. Of all state prisoners 62% were convicted of nonviolent crimes, and of all federal prisoners 75% were in for nonviolent crimes.[9] John Augustus' clients also were mostly poor, unemployed, drunkards, that is, had a substance abuse problem and were mostly nonviolent. Based on the types of people that are in prison and in light of the success of John Augustus' work, alternative sanctions would be more effective in dealing with most of today's prison population. Peacemaking criminologists would and do support alternatives to incarceration. Alternative sanctions such as halfway houses, drug rehabilitation outside of prison, community service and civic restitution are similar to the kinds of methods that Augustus applied to his clients.

Many studies examine alternatives to incarceration, albeit in the few cases in the United States where alternatives are used, and present the following findings: Alternatives to incarceration 1) are cheaper than prison; 2) have lower rates of recidivism than incarceration; 3) are tougher, more demanding and more rigorous than having nonviolent offenders sitting around in prisons and learning lessons from dangerous violent inmates; and 4) relieve overcrowding and provide more room to put away dangerous offenders who need to be separated from society.[10] Moreover, research indicates that drug rehabilitation, community service work, civic restitution and halfway houses would increase public safety.[11] The research clearly demonstrates the failure of today's prisons, as well as during John Augustus' time, in dealing with many types of crime (in particular, people with drug or alcohol problems), and this research indicates the effectiveness of alternative sanctions in cases involving nonviolent crimes.[12]

Considering that most prisoners in America are convicted of nonviolent crimes and were unemployed and/or poor at the time of their arrest, a full time employment bill would logically prevent many types of crimes. Today, by comparison, Scandinavian countries as well as Japan and Holland have low unemployment rates (close to 0% unemployment) and have very low crime rates and very low imprisonment rates.[13] Part of John Augustus' success was that he found employment for many of his clients. The employment of his clients played a role in the success of their rehabilitation.[14] Peacemaking criminologists, expanding on Augustus' work and in their efforts to prevent suffering, would support the implementation of a full employment bill, a non-violent, non-authoritarian and humane way to prevent crime.

America's prison system, as one of the world's largest and most costly prison systems, contains 1.2 million people at a cost of over 30 billion dollars a year.[15] Research indicates the ineffectiveness of incarceration by showing there is no association between spending money to incarcerate more people and a lower crime rate.[16] For instance, even though the U. S. maintains such a high imprisonment rate, America still has the highest crime rate among industrialized nations.[17] A peacemaking criminological approach is needed to cut the crime rate in the United States. As we have seen, John Augustus' work was quite successful and exemplified the principles of peacemaking criminology. The implementation of alternative sanctions and a full employment bill is a continuation and expansion of John Augustus' successful work and would be supported by peacemaking criminology. In conclusion, based on the data presented in this chapter, the crime and recidivism rates in America would decline as an outcome of the development and growth of a peacemaking criminological viewpoint.

NOTES

1. Originally published as Louis Gesualdi, "The Work of John Augustus: Peacemaking Criminology," *Academy of Criminal Justice Sciences ACJS Today* 17, no. 3 (1999): 1, 3-4 and see Victor Kappeler, Mark Blumberg, Gary Potter. *The Mythology of Crime and Criminal Justice* (Illinois: Waveland Press, 1996).

2. John R. Fuller, *Criminal Justice: A Peacemaking Perspective* (Boston: Allyn and Bacon, 1998).

3. Harold E. Pepinsky and Richard Quinney, eds., *Criminology as Peacemaking,* (Bloomington: Indiana University Press, 1991).

4. Fuller, *Criminal Justice: A Peacemaking Perspective.*

5. John Augustus, *John Augustus: First Probation Officer* (New Jersey: Patterson Smith, 1972).

6. Ibid 1-23.

7. Ibid, 23.

8. Ibid, 31.

9. Peter T. Elikann. *The Tough on Crime Myth* (New York: Insight Books, 1996).

10. Ibid.

11. Ibid.

12. Ibid.

13. Ibid, 32-34.

14. Augustus, *John Augustus: First Probation Officer,* 1972.

15. Elikann. *The Tough on Crime Myth,* 47-49.

16. Ibid.

17. Kappeler, Blumberg, and Potter, *The Mythology of Crime and Criminal Justice,* 1996.

4

The Future of the U.S. Healthcare System

A Peacemaking View

Peacemaking Criminology argues that the following main components, listed below, are needed in a future model of the U.S. Healthcare System.

- Appropriate attention on wellness and the prevention of disease.
- The attainment to primary care for everyone.
- The combination of talents and expertise of all trained healthcare professionals
- Better-quality health results
- Control of health care costs.[1]

A peacemaking view points out that the U.S. Healthcare System need to deal with the following workforce challenges.

- Dealing with a lack of health care professionals.
- Unifying the abilities and knowhow of qualified professionals in a way that alleviates shortages.
- Permitting nurses to practice in a manner that employs their education and training.
- The integration of licensing rules across states to develop more innovative trained nurses.
- Nurses to be educated in community health, public health, and geriatrics.
- Teaching in geriatrics for all health care professionals.
- Teaching primary care physicians to be wide-ranging.
- Improving social know-how among all health care professionals.[2]

A peacemaking view argues that the best way to make the necessary changes listed above is to set up a universal healthcare in the United States. The following reasons are listed for the setting up of universal healthcare in our country.

- The United States has the highest use of the most illicit drugs in the world (see chapters 3 and 5 of this book).
- The number of deaths due to Covid 19 is noticeable higher in the United States than most other countries in the world. The US healthcare system did and does not deal with the Covid 19 crisis very well. Over a million individuals have died and still are dying in the U.S. due to covid. Western Europe, South Korea, Japan and others dealt with Covid 19 better than the United States and these countries have a universal healthcare system.[3]
- The people of over 30 countries in the world live longer than the USA. These 30 countries include the countries in Western Europe, South Korea and Japan which all have a universal healthcare system.[4]

NOTES

1. See Leiyu Shi and Douglas A. Singh, *Essentials of the U.S. Health Care System* (Burlington, MA: Jones & Bartlett Learning Books) 2023.
2. Ibid.
3. www.thinkglobalhealth.org.
4. World Data. Info.

5

Peacemaking Acts and Programs to Cut Adult and Teen Crime

There is a pattern to the persons incarcerated in the United States. Thirty-five percent were unemployed at the time of their arrest and most of those who had been working had very low-paying jobs. Drug offenders represent the largest proportional growth of inmates increasing from 8% of the prison population in the early 1980s to approximately 25% in the late 1990s. Of all state prisoners, 62% were convicted of nonviolent crimes, and of all federal prisoners, 75% were in for nonviolent crimes.[1]

America presently maintains, among the world's democratic nations, the largest and most expensive prison system, with approximately 1.5 million people at a cost of over 30 billion dollars a year. For every 100,000 people in the U.S., 600 were behind bars in 1997. By way of comparison, Great Britain incarcerated 100 out of 100,000; Italy, 85; Japan, 37; and Holland, 65.[2] Moreover, the federal prison system in America was operating at 46 percent over capacity and state prisons were 31 percent over capacity.[3] Research indicates the ineffectiveness of incarceration by showing there is no association between money spent to incarcerate and a reduced rate of crime among adults and teenagers.[4] For instance, even though the U.S. maintains the highest imprisonment rate among the world's democratic nations, America still has the highest adult and teen crime rate among these nations.[5]

The purpose of this chapter is to present political acts and programs from a peacemaking approach to criminology that may very well reverse this situation. A peacemaking perspective to criminology, as stated previously, is a humanistic approach to criminology. This approach views crime as just one of the many forms of suffering (such as war, poverty, unemployment and others) that characterize human existence. It is involved with the advancement of humane, non violent, non-authoritarian and scientific ways to reduce (and eventually end) suffering and oppression. A peacemaking viewpoint proposes major changes in the social and economic structures in the United States so that they no longer bring about suffering and oppression.[6]

A peacemaking approach to criminology would campaign for and support the following political acts and programs: 1) a full employment bill, 2) a real minimum wage, 3) a nationalized health care bill, 4) a bill ending the prohibition of drugs, and 5) the implementation of intermediate sanctions. The adult and teen crime rates as well as recidivism rates in America would probably decline significantly as an outcome of these acts and programs.

First, since most prisoners in America were convicted of nonviolent crimes, were unemployed and/or poor at the time of their arrest, a full time employment bill and a real minimum wage (that is, a salary that would provide a good standard of living) would logically, and in a humane way, prevent many types of crimes. Other countries, unlike the U.S., (such as the Scandinavian countries, Japan, Holland) that have low unemployment rates (close to 0% unemployment) and a good standard of living (this includes good housing, health care and educational opportunities for the population at large) have very low crime rates and very low imprisonment rates.[7]

Violent youth crime and adult crime in America are due to poverty. American social policies force 25% of our youth to grow up in poverty leading to high rates of violence not found in other Western nations. Specifically, America raises three to eight times more children in poverty than other Western nations.[8]

A full time employment bill and a real minimum wage would provide poor adults and poor teens with a real chance to better their lives. In fact, such a bill and wage would not only be beneficial to the poor but probably to almost all Americans.

Second, ending the prohibition of drugs and a nationalized health care bill are needed in dealing with the drug problem in the U.S. The reasoning behind this argument is that drug decriminalization and nationalized health care became public policy in Holland, and drug use dropped considerably in that country. Specifically, the consumption of marijuana in the Netherlands has decreased from 10 percent of the population in 1976 to around 3 percent in the 1990s. The percentage of people using marijuana in Holland is considerably less than in the United States where marijuana possession in many states is still illegal.[9] Also, in the Netherlands, decriminalized cocaine is used by 1200 percent fewer people than in the United States.[10] Drug use dropped significantly in Holland because of educational and rehabilitation programs that are part of nationalized health care. Law enforcement did not play a role in this very significant decline of drug use.

America's drug strategy, on the other hand, which is based on law enforcement (that is, the war on drugs), has only been effective in increasing the numbers of arrests, convictions and imprisonment. It has failed in reducing drug abuse and addiction.[11] Recent research presents the following facts: 1) Presently, cocaine is inexpensive and more abundant than ever, 2) emergency room visits are high across the U.S. for adverse reactions to drugs, 3) teen drug use is very high, and 4) the number of people most in need of drug treatment is large.[12]

The problem with America's current drug strategy "lies with spending most of the money on law enforcement and interdiction (supply) and too small an amount on rehabilitation and preventive education (demand)."[13] For instance, although the United States "spends more than 50 million dollars a year on research to prevent crime, 15 billion dollars is spent annually on drug enforcement."[14]

Research shows that "treatment is more effective in cutting drug use than law enforcement."[15] For instance, a 1997 study by RAND's Drug Policy Research Center concluded that treatment (rehabilitation) is the most effective tool in the fight against drug abuse, finding that rehabilitation reduces 15 times more serious crime than mandatory minimum sentences. Moreover, several studies sponsored by the National Institute on Drug Abuse have shown that drug rehabilitation programs on the whole are successful in reducing the levels of drug abuse and crime among participants (adults and teens) and in increasing their ability to hold a job. Furthermore, drug treatment costs less than imprisonment. For instance, in New York State the cost of most drug-free outpatient care runs about $2,700 - $3,600 per person per year, and the cost of residential drug treatment is $17,000-$20,000 per participant per year.[16] These expenses are way less than keeping an inmate in a New York State prison at an approximate cost of $30,000 a year.[17]

Overall, studies indicate that drug laws make the drug problems among adults and teens in the United States worse. There are also other benefits to be derived by ending the prohibition of drugs. Repealing drug laws will save at least 17 billion dollars a year in law enforcement, and organized crime groups would be dealt a severe setback.[18] Therefore, Americans need to view the drug problem as more of a public health issue than a criminal justice system problem.[19]

Third, prisons are mainly needed to separate dangerous violent offenders from society in order to rehabilitate them and not as a primary form of correction. Intermediate sanctions or alternatives to incarceration are more humane and effective ways to deal with nonviolent adult and teen offenders. These alternatives include community service, drug rehabilitation outside prison, halfway houses and civic restitution.

Many studies examine alternatives to incarceration and present the following findings: 1) Alternatives to incarceration are cheaper than prison; 2) they have lower rates of recidivism than incarceration; 3) intermediate sanctions are tougher, more demanding and more rigorous than having nonviolent adult and teen offenders sitting around in prisons and learning lessons from dangerous violent inmates; 4) they relieve overcrowding and provide more room to put away dangerous offenders who need to be separated from society.[20] Moreover, research indicates that drug rehabilitation (as part of nationalized health care), community service work, civic restitution and halfway houses would increase public safety. The research demonstrates the failure of the incarceration of offenders in dealing with offenses (in particular, nonviolent offenses) and clearly describes the effectiveness of alternatives to prison for nonviolent offenses in general.[21]

The criminal justice system in the United States has developed and enforced unnecessary laws (drug laws), harsh punishment (nonviolent offenders in prison), and has misplaced social resources (money spent to imprison people). It has failed to deal with many societal problems and adult and teen offenders in the United States.

In conclusion, a peacemaking approach to criminology could not only support the implementation of different intermediate sanctions but also changes in the social and economic structures of American society. These changes, as stated previously, would include a full employment bill, a real minimum wage, nationalized health care and ending the prohibition of drugs. Such political acts and programs would provide adult and teen offenders rehabilitation and a real chance to better their lives.

NOTES

1. This chapter originally published as Louis Gesualdi, "Peacemaking Acts and Programs to Cut Adult and Teen Crime," *Sociological Viewpoints* 19, (2003): 7-10. Also, see Victor Kappeler, Mark Blumberg, and Gary Potter, *The Mythology of Crime and Criminal Justice* (Illinois, Waveland Press, 2000): 158 and Elikann, *The Tough on Crime Myth* (New York: Insight Books, 1996): 50-51, 162.

2. See Kappeler, Blumberg and Potter. *The Mythology of Crime and Criminal Justice* and Elikann. *The Tough on Crime Myth.*

3. See Elikann. *The Tough on Crime Myth* and Bureau of Justice Statistics, U.S. Department of Justice, "Jail Inmates, 1993-1994," April, 1995.

4. See Mike Males, *Framing Youth: Ten Myths about the Next Generation* (Maine: Common Courage Press, 1999), and *The Scapegoat Generation: America's War on Adolescent* (Maine: Common Courage Press, 1996), and Elikann. *The Tough on Crime Myth*, 127-145.

5. See Kappeler, Blumberg and Potter, *The Mythology of Crime and Criminal Justice*, Males, *Framing Youth,* and *The Scapegoat Generation*, and Steven F. Messner and Richard Rosenfeld, *Crime and the American Dream* (California: Wadsworth Inc., 1994).

6. See Harold Pepinsky and Richard Quinney, eds., *Criminology as Peacemaking* (Bloomington: Indiana University Press, 1991).

7. Elikann. *The Tough on Crime Myth*, 32-44.

8. Males. *The Scapegoat Generation.*

9. Kappeler, Blumberg and Potter, *The Mythology of Crime and Criminal Justice*, Jonathan Blank, *Sex, Drugs and Democracy,* Film Documentary, 1994, Netherlands: Red Hat Productions (DVD), 2001, and Arnold Trebach and Eddy Engelman, "Why Not Decriminalize?," *New Perspective Quarterly,* 1989.

10. See Trebach and Engelman, "Why Not Decriminalize?"

11. See Elikann, *The Tough on Crime Myth*, 163.

12. Ibid, 163-164.

13. Ibid, 168-169.

14. Ibid, 15.

15. See Elikann, *The Tough on Crime Myth*, 13, and Correctional Association of New York, New York, NY, 1998.

16. *Correctional Association of New York,* New York, NY, 1998.

17. Ibid.

18. See Kappeler, Blumberg, and Potter. *The Mythology of Crime and Criminal Justice,* 171-172 and Ethan A. Nadelmann, "Drug Prohibition in the United States: Costs, Consequences, and Alternatives," *Science* 245, no. 4921 (1989).

19. See Kappeler, Blumberg and Potter. *The Mythology of Crime and Criminal Justice*, 143-172.

20. Elikann. *The Tough on Crime Myth*, 14.

21. See Kappeler, Blumberg and Potter. *The Mythology of Crime and Criminal Justice*, and Elikann. *The Tough on Crime Myth*.

6

Popularly Held Beliefs about Italian Americans and Organized Crime

Peacemaking Critique

As we begin the third decade of the twenty-first century, as a society, we like to think of our civilization progressing and modernizing; especially through globalization. However, I am disappointed to say that disturbing and popularly held beliefs about Italian Americans and organized crime in the United States still exist. In fact, there is a continually high percentage of Americans who disapprove of this group. Therefore, to examine progress in society, this chapter examines the stigmas held about Italian Americans and organized crime. Second, this chapter presents data that shows a more accurate depiction of this ethnic group with some recommendations to improve relations with Italian Americans.[1] In other words, this chapter represents a peacemaking view of crime and criminology by its examination of the misinformation on crime and criminal justice (stigmas held about Italian Americans and organized crime) and its presentation of a more accurate picture of criminal behavior (data presented that shows a more accurate depiction of Italian Americans).

One of the reasons for the negative portrayal of Italian Americans can be seen in S. Robert Lichter and Daniel R. Amundon's report *Portrayal of Italian American Characters in Prime Television Series 1994-1995*. These authors show that Italian Americans are rarely seen as heroes or even in a high status role on television. The study also shows evidence of popular culture's continuing association of Italian Americans with organized crime.[2] This can also be seen in Bill Dal Cerro's research *Italian Culture on Film*

1928-1999 (1999) which analyzes how Italian Americans are portrayed in movies over a 70-year period. Results of the research reveal a consistent negative portrayal of Italian/Americans (that is 74% of the films involving Italian/Americans). What is meant by negative portrayal in popular culture are movies dealing with Italian/Americans, images of Italian/Americans as violent criminals predominate (41%), followed by portrayals of boors, buffoons, bigots and other social undesirables (33%).[3] Presently, media bias still persists. In 2015 the Italic Institute of America, "Film Study 2015 (1914 -2014)" found that almost 70 percent of Italian related films produced from 1914 to 2014 portrayed Italians in a negative light. The Institute also provides a list of more recent media releases that contain negative portrayals of Italians. The list includes cartoons, games, books, television shows, movies and several remakes that turned an unidentified villain into a villain with an Italian surname.[4] These figures clearly indicate an entrenched, institutionalized bias against Americans of Italian descent in the entertainment industry.

The National Public Opinion Research for Commission for Social Justice Order Sons of Italy in America's study *Americans of Italian Descent: A Study of Public Images, Beliefs and Misperceptions* reports that 74% of the U.S. public sees Italian Americans associated with organized crime.[5] Richard A. Capozzola's work *Finalmente: The Truth about Organized Crime* suggests that the media and politicians, by exaggerating the role of Italian Americans in organized crime, have influenced the public's inaccurate and negative perception of this ethnic group. This exaggeration can be seen in the suggestion that Italian Americans developed organized crime in the United States and that a significant percentage of Italian Americans are involved in the Mafia.[6]

Unfortunately, due to the negative portrayal of Italian Americans, a self-fulfilling prophecy begins to develop within their own group. This can be seen in Zogby International's *National Survey: American Teenagers and Stereotyping* which reveals that teens learn the less admirable aspects of their heritage from entertainment industry stereotyping. The Report indicates that 46% of Italian American teens said that television's portrayal of Italian Americans as crime bosses is accurate and 30% said that they were proud of their TV image. Moreover, the Report shows that 78 percent of all American teenagers associate Italian Americans with criminal activities.[7] In addition, another study revealed that a significant percent of all Americans in all age groups feel that all Italian Americans are connected to the mob. [8]

These recent studies indicate that Italian Americans are still portrayed and perceived as being involved in criminality and socially undesirable behavior. Moreover, these studies show that many Americans believe Italian Americans developed organized crime in the United States and that a significant percentage of Italian Americans are involved in the Mafia. However, peace-making criminologists, through social scientific studies, do not support these commonly held beliefs about Italian Americans. This chapter, through social scientific studies, will now present a more accurate representation of Italian Americans.

First, research points out that Italian Americans did not develop organized crime in the United States. H. Abadinsky's book *Organized Crime* (1985) points out that organized crime existed in the United States before the arrival of the large numbers of Italian immigrants from 1880 to 1920. This study discusses the negative practices by such famous nineteenth century businessmen as John Jacob Astor, Cornelius Vanderbilt, John D. Rockefeller, and others. Such practices included extortion, blackmail, violence, bribery, murder, and the use of thugs and private armies to destroy a competitor. This work verifies that the practices of the nineteenth century businessmen were no different from the practices of Italian American gangsters of the 20th century. Moreover, the book indicates that the social, economic, historical and cultural conditions in the United States produced organized crime.[9]

Second, D. Cauchon's article "Head of BCCI-linked Bank Quits,"[10] A. Block and F. Scarpitti's book *Poisoning for Profit: The Mafia and Toxic Waste*[11] and W. Chambliss' study *On the Take: From Petty Crooks to Presidents*[12] detail the huge involvement of the police, big businesses, and the CIA in the development of organized crime groups. In addition, J. Mills' book *The Underground Empire: Where Crime and Government Embrace* presents evidence revealing that the United States government has been a major player in international drug crime systems.[13] These works show the role that the government (including the CIA and the police) and big business have played in the growth of organized crime in the U.S.

Third, V. Kappeler, M. Blumberg, and G. Potter's book *The Mythology of Crime and Criminal Justice* describes the prevalent practices employed by the media, law enforcement personnel, and government officials to manipulate information and create crime myths. Some of these practices involve creating criminal stereotypes, interjecting personal opinion into media presentation without factual basis; presenting certain facts and not others; and presenting supposedly factual information with undocumented sources of authority. Their work indicates that the media, law enforcement personnel and government officials have used such practices to blame Italian Americans for developing organized crime. Furthermore, Kappeler, Blumberg, and Potter's book convincingly argues that the socioeconomic conditions of American society need to be investigated in order to understand the cause of organized crime.[14]

Data indicate that contrary to popular belief a significant percentage of Italian Americans are not involved in the Mafia. As a matter of fact, only a fraction of 1 percent of all Italian Americans participate in organized crime.[15]

According to the Federal Bureau of Investigation, there were allegedly 5,000 Italian American who were made members of the Mafia at the height of involvement. Currently, according to the FBI, there are 1,500 Italian Americans who are members of the Mafia out of 20 million Italian Americans. Furthermore, of an estimated 500,000 members of organized crime in America today, Italian Americans make up a slim 0.3 percent of all involved.[16]

In short, the evidence demonstrates that the widely held beliefs about Italians are unfounded. Italian Americans did not develop organized crime in the United States and only a fraction of a percent of all Italian Americans participates in organized crime. In addition, social scientific research points out social, economic, historical and cultural factors of American society gave rise to organized crime. This is something that needs to be addressed and studied further in order to prevent future increases in crime rates while increasing our standard of living.

The reasons, according to this author, for blaming Italian Americans for organized crime are as follows. First, the media finds Italian American organized crime stories profitable. Second, some politicians, especially when their opponent is Italian American, find associating Italian Americans with organized crime useful for winning votes.

It is this author's opinion that as long as the above and widely held belief about Italian Americans and organized crime continues to exist in the United States, organized crime will not be dealt with properly. Kappeler, Blumberg, and Potter's *The Mythology of Crime and Criminal Justice* indicates that the media, law enforcement personnel and the U.S. government need to be held accountable for the blaming of a single ethnic group for the development of organized crime in the United States.[17] Moreover, law enforcement agencies, big businesses and the government need to take responsibility for their part in participating in many organized activities. For instance, David R. Simon's book *Elite Deviance* examines the institutionalized set of deviant practices by elites (persons form the highest strata of U.S. society) that are international. His book points out these elites' collaboration with organized crime involved in the 850 billion dollar global narcotics trade and the vast amount of money laundered by legitimate financial institutions, lawyers and other elite professionals.[18]

To deal with organized crime more successfully according to this author, it makes sense to think of organized crime as a business that provides illegal goods and services, rather than an Italian or alien conspiracy. It needs to be recognized that organized crime is able to flourish primarily because of the high demand for goods and services (for instance, drugs) that have been designated as illegal.

Moreover, efforts need to focus on identifying and dealing with political, corporate and financial deviance that serves as links between the underworld and upper world. For example, Stephen M. Rossoff, Henry W. Pontell and Robert Tillman's book *Profit without Honor: White Collar Crime and the Looting of America* points out that corrupt banks are central to the operations of organized crime that import billions of dollars of illegal drugs into the U.S.[19]

In conclusion, peacemaking criminology, through recent studies, indicates that Italian Americans are inaccurately portrayed and misperceived as being involved in criminality and socially undesirable behavior. Moreover, peacemaking criminology, through social scientific research, shows organized crime is able to flourish primarily because of the high demand for goods and services that have been designated as illegal and not because it is an Italian or alien conspiracy.

Finally, this chapter makes the following recommendations based on R. A. Capozzola's *Finalmente: The Truth about Organized Crime)*[20] and Carol Chiago Lujinnos' study "The Only Real Indian is the Stereotyped Indian,"[21] to deal with the incorrect, negative representations and misunderstanding of Italian Americans, as previously stated. First, more Italian Americans need to support and participate in such organizations as the Order Sons of Italy in America, the National Italian American Foundation and Unico National. Second, more Italian Americans need to voice their protests, concerns, or objections by phoning or writing to radio stations, television networks, newspapers, and magazines that offend their group as well as other groups. Third, more Italian Americans need to hold accountable politicians, actors, celebrities, and writers who portraying Italian Americans, as well as other groups, falsely and negatively. Fourth, more Italian Americans need to boycott movies, TV shows, products and businesses that offend their group as well as other groups. Fifth, more Italian Americans need to speak up when someone is saying something that is inaccurate and offensive about their group and about other groups. Sixth, long-term efforts to reduce negative stereotyping of Italian Americans include establishing and supporting Italian American studies programs at both state and privately funded educational institutions. Seventh, books and other publications in law, government, history, and the social sciences need to include a more widespread analysis of the Italian American experience. Eighth, Italian Americans need to become more noticeable and concerned in politics, law and education, as well as in other leadership ranks, to support a more truthful representation of Italian Americans. A peacemaking approach to crime and criminal justice agrees with the above recommendations.

NOTES

1. This chapter is an updated version of a chapter that was published in Louis Gesualdi, *The Italian American Experience: A Collection of Writings* (Lanham, Maryland: University Press of America, 2012).

2. S. Robert Lichter and Daniel R. Amundon, *Portrayal of Italian American Character in Prime Television Series, 1994-1995,* Washington, D.C.: Social Justice Order Sons of Italy, 1996.

3. Bill Dal Cerro, *Italian Culture on Film, 1928-1999,* Floral Park, NY: Italic Studies Institute Image Research Project, 1999.

4. Janice Therese Mancuso, "Searching for Italian American History" (paper) presented at the American

Italian Sociohistorical Association First Conference Series entitled *The Italian American Experience: A Sociohistorical Examination* held at St. John's University, Queens, NY on October 21, 2015. Also, see Italic Institute of America, "Film Study 2015 (1914-2014)," italic.org/media watch/film study. Php, 2015, and see Italic

Institute of America, "Exhibit A: Examples of Media, Bias, "italic.org/anti-defamation/Exhibit A.php, 2015.

5. *Americans of Italian Decent: A Study of Public Images, Beliefs and Misperceptions,* Washington, D.C.: The National Public Opinion Research Commission for Social Justice Order Sons of Italy, 1991.

6. Richard A. Capozzola, *Finalmente: The Truth about Organized Crime,* Altamonte Springs, FL.: Five Centuries Books, 2001.

7. Zogby International, *National Survey: American Teenagers and Stereotyping,* Utica, NY: Zogby International, 2001.

8. See M. Alfano, "Negative Stereotype Persist though FBI Figures Reveal Facts," *ComUnico Magazine,* April 2002.

9. Howard Abadinsky, *Organized Crime,* Chicago, IL: Nelson Hall, 1985.

10. D. Cauchon, "Head of BCCI-Link Bank Quits," *USA Today,* August 15, 1991.

11. A. Block and F. Scarpitti, *Poisoning for Profit: The Mafia and Toxic Waste,* New York, NY: William Morrow, 1985.

12. William Chambliss, *On the Take: From Petty Crooks to Presidents,* Bloomington: Indiana University Press, 1978.

13. J. Mills, *The Underground Empire: Where Crime and Government Embrace,* New York: Doubleday, 1986.

14. Victor Kappeler, Mark Blumberg and Gary Potter. *The Mythology of Crime and Criminal Justice,* Illinois: Waveland Press, 2000.

15. Richard Gambino, "America's Most Tolerated Intolerance: Bigotry against Italian Americans," *The Italian American Review* (Spring/Summer) 1997.

16. M. Alfano, "Negative Stereotype Persist though FBI Figures Reveal Facts," *ComUnico Magazine,* April 2002.

17. Victor Kappeler, Mark Blumberg and Gary Potter. *The Mythology of Crime and Criminal Justice,* Illinois: Waveland Press, 2000.

18. D. Simon, *Elite Deviance,* Boston: Allyn and Bacon, 1999.

19. Stephen M. Rossoff, Henry W. Pontell and Robert H. Tillman, *Profit without Honor: White-Collar*
  Crime and the Looting of America, New Jersey: Pearson Education, Inc., 2002.

20. Richard A. Capozzola, *Finalmente: The Truth about Organized Crime,* Altamonte Springs, FL.: Five Centuries Books, 2001.

21. Carol Chiago Lujinnos, "The Only Real Indian is the Stereotyped Indian" in Coramae Richey Mann and Marjorie S. Zatz (eds.) *Images of Color Images of Crime,* CA: Roxbury Publishing Co., 1998.

7

A Peacemaking Approach Dealing
with the Criminal Elite

Peacemaking Criminology examines the harmful acts committed by the well-off. Such acts include embezzlement, bribery, computer crimes, crimes against the consumer (fraud, unsafe products), medical crimes, and environmental crimes (pollution, unsafe workplaces). In its analysis of these harmful acts, peacemaking criminology points out the bias against the poor that exist within America's criminal justice system.[1]

A peacemaking perspective to crime indicates that the acts in which poor people harm others (theft, assault, murder) are treated as serious crimes, while harmful acts for which well-off people are responsible for are not treated as serious crimes (and many times are not treated as crimes at all). This perspective notes that harmful acts by the well-off oftentimes are a substantially greater hazard to the public than harmful acts by the poor. For instance, unsafe workplaces, unsafe products, medical crimes and pollution lead to far more misery, far more dying and disability, and cost more money than all the murders, aggravated assaults and thefts that are reported each year by the FBI.[2]

The criminal justice system, according to a peacemaking view, tends to treat well-off offenders who are guilty of fraud, embezzlement, bribery and computer crimes more kindly than poor offenders who are guilty of nonviolent property crime. A peacemaking view states that the well-off offenders are less likely to be arrested, prosecuted and incarcerated than poor offenders, even when they have committed the same offense. Also, this view asserts the failure of the criminal justice system in reducing the large amount of dangerous offenses committed in American society.[3]

Peacemaking criminology makes the following recommendations to protect the public from crime and advance justice.

- Policies need to be developed to eliminate poverty.
- Criminal justice needs to establish and execute punishments that fit the
  hurtfulness of the offense without regard to the class of the offender.
- American society needs to make lawful the production and sale of illicit
  drugs and deal with addiction as a medical challenge.
- Rehabilitation programs need to be developed in order to promote personal responsibility.
- Ex-offenders need to be offered training and a chance to succeed as law-
  abiding citizens.
- The range in which police officers, prosecutors, and judges exercise
  discretion needs to be restricted, and the development of policies to hold
  these law enforcers liable to the public for their decisions is necessary.
- American society has to enact a more just apportioning of wealth and
  income and to make equal opportunity a reality for everyone.[4]

A peacemaking approach to crime makes evident that white-collar crimes
and corporate crimes are a substantially greater hazard to the public than
street crimes. White-collar crimes include bribery, fraud, kickbacks, payoffs,
computer crimes, consumer fraud, illegal competition, deceptive practices,
embezzlement, receiving stolen property, securities theft and tax evasion.
Corporate crimes include pollution, unsafe workplaces and unsafe products.
According to a peacemaking approach, all other forms of criminal behavior
in U.S. society do not commence to be equivalent to the costs, in terms of
both money and human lives, of white-collar and corporate crimes.[5] The
total monetary damage from white-collar and corporate crime is estimated
to be anywhere from $231 billion to over a trillion dollars a year, whereas
street crime is estimated to be $15 billion to $20 billion a year. As of 2021,
annual losses from white-collar crimes are anywhere from $426 billion to
$1.7 trillion dollars. In addition, each year, an estimated 200,000, people die
and 20,000,000 more are seriously injured from corporate crime that is an
outcome of pollution, unsafe workplaces and unsafe products. In contrast,
approximated 23,000 murders and 850,000 assaults are committed in the
streets each year in the United States. Street crime, according to peacemaking

criminology, is less of a threat, less of a danger, and less of a burden to society than white-collar and corporate crimes. [6]

Peacemaking criminology asserts that the social cost of white-collar crime (institutional corruption) involves an erosion of trust that Americans place in big business, the government, the medical profession and religious organizations. Such a lack of trust by the public due to institutional corruption, according to peacemaking criminology, encourages and promotes other types of crimes. A peacemaking to crime and criminal justice proclaims that the continuation of elite wrongdoing endorses a lack of respect by potential and street criminals pursuing to validate their misbehavior.[7] Moreover, peacemaking criminology states that crooked banks are crucial to the acts of international cartels that import billions of dollars of drugs into the United States of America.[8]

A peacemaking view to crime and criminal justice present a number of suggestions for controlling white-collar and corporate crimes. First, new laws are needed to impose tougher penalties for controlling white-collar and corporate crimes. Second, a system of regulatory codes and administrative agencies need to be created to monitor corporate conduct and respond to criminal violations. Third, there is a need to develop internationally agreed upon standard of conduct in dealing with white collar and corporate crime. Fourth, the American public has to show less tolerance to those convicted of white-collar and corporate crimes.[9]

Peacemaking criminology points out that there exist respected men and women employing the most unethical methods to increase already abundant wealth, the lack of concern by many large corporations to the injuries and deaths they caused innocent people, in fractions of human rights by the U.S. government, and the deficiency and corruption of law enforcement[10]

NOTES

1. Jeffrey Reiman and Paul Leighton. *The Rich Get Richer and the Poor Get Prison: Ideology, Class and Criminal Justice,* New York, NY: Routledge, 2023.
2. Ibid.
3. Ibid.
4. Ibid.
5. See Victor E. Kappeler and Gary W. Potter. *The Mythology of Crime and Criminal Justice,* Long Grove, IL:

Waveland Press, 2018 and see Stephen M. Rosoff, Henry N. Pontell and Robert Tillman, *Profits without Honor*

White-Collar Crime and the Looting of America, Upper Saddle River, NJ: Pearson, 2019. Also, see James William Coleman. *The Criminal Elite: Understanding White-Collar Crime*, New York, NY: Worth Publishers, 20005, see www.zippia .com and see www.fincancierworldwide.com.

6. Ibid.

7. See Rosoff, Pontell, and Tillman's *Profit without Honor: White-Collar Crime and the Looting of America,* 2018.

8. Ibid.

9. Ibid.

10. See Coleman's. *The Criminal Elite: Understanding White-Collar Crime*, 2005.

8

Human Capitalism

Capitalism, according to Andrew Yang's research, tends to undervalue many things, activities, and people, many of which are core to the human experience. Below is listed the many things, activities and people that tend to be undervalued by the market economy.[1]

- Caring for loved ones
- Educating or raising children
- Arts and creativeness
- Helping the poor
- The ecological unit or environment
- Reading
- Preventive health care
- Honor and integrity
- Infrastructure and freely available transportation
- Reporting
- Womenfolk
- People of color/underrepresented minorities

And in this day and age, progressively more,

- Unskillful work and common people
- Important unrestricted contacts
- Small self-determining businesses
- Good and efficient government

Yang's research asserts that today's market economy needs to shift focus on improving the lot of the average person. His work refers to this shift as Human Capitalism and indicates that Human Capitalism would have a few core tenets (listed below).[2]

1. Humanity is more important than money.
2. The unit of an economy is each person, not each dollar.
3. Markets exist to serve our common goals and values.

Peacemaking criminology agrees with Andrew Yang's work that capitalism as is, tends to undervalue many things, activities and people which are core to the human experience. Also, peacemaking criminology, in agreement with Yang's book, supports the development of Human Capitalism. Human Capitalism asserts that the market economy needs to focus on improving the lot in life of the average person and that capitalism needs to be compelled to serve human ends and goals, rather than have our humanity diminished to serve the marketplace. Human beings, according to Human Capitalism, make the system and possess it, not the other way around.[3]

NOTES

1. See Andrew Yang, *The War on Normal People*, New York, NY: Hachette Books, 2018, pages 197-204.
2. Ibid.
3. Ibid.

9

Social Characteristics that Favor the Development of Creative Genius

A Peacemaking View

Silvanno Arieti's Socio-historical Book *Creativity: The Magic Synthesis* indicates the social characteristics that favor the development of creative genius in a society. A peacemaking view of criminology, as a movement, supports the development of such a society. Arieti's work points out the following characteristics that support the development of creative genius in a society.[1]

- A society is willing to advance technological knowledge and cultivate a tradition in music, science, and/or art.
- A society is eager to be open to and inspires creative effort.
- A culture is enthusiastic to stress "becoming, not just being," change and the future, not just instant pleasure.
- A society is agreeable to have all citizens, not just the few, entrance to the creative arts.
- A society is prepared to offer groups that have been traditionally oppressed more freedom. Both the past oppression and the new found freedom come together to heighten creative contributions.
- A society is ready to be open to cultural diversities.
- A society is eager to tolerate differing interpretations and will give the unfamiliar an opportunity.
- A society is willing to be in favor of creative people interacting with each other.
- A society is prepared to make available enticements and rewards for individuals who are creative.[2]

In conclusion, it is a society that allows or not allows creative genius to develop. Many people are potentially creative geniuses, but actual geniuses are not randomly distributed in the world because some societies support them while others stifle them.[3] A peacemaking view of criminology supports the social characteristics that favor the advancement of creative genius in a society.

NOTES

1. Silvano Arieti. *Creativity. The Magic Synthesis.* New York: Basic Books, 1976 and Joel M. Charon *Sociology: A Conceptual Approach.* Boston: Allyn and Bacon, 1989.
2. Ibid.
3. Ibid.

10

A Development of Economic Democracy

There have been many consequences as a result of the global expansion of the market economy over the last thirty years. Positive consequences include tremendous developments in communication, transportation and technology that produce great amounts of goods and services. However, there have been negative consequences because of the expansion of the market economy, including the following:

- The majority of the world's toxic wastes (produced by highly techno-logical developed countries) are dumped in third world countries in an unsafe, hazardous manner.[1]
- Since 1970, the world's forests have declined from 4.4 square miles per 1000 people to 2.8 square miles per 1000.
- A quarter of the world's fish stock has been depleted or is in danger of being depleted and another 44 percent are being fished at their biological limit.[2]
- 36 of the world's 40 poorest countries export food to North America.
- In Africa, half the population suffers from protein deficiencies, and yet, they export protein foods to Europe.[3]
- The average African household today consumes 20 percent less than it did 25 years ago.
- The world's 225 richest individuals, of whom 60 are Americans with total assets of $311 billion, have a combined wealth of over $1 trillion–equal to the annual income of the poorest 47 percent of the entire world's population.[4]

- More and more work is exported to Third World countries because the work is often hazardous. These countries are low wage havens for big businesses, and they guarantee no interference from health and safety regulations.[5]
- Air, water and land throughout the world are being poisoned due to exported work by big businesses.
- Unemployment and poverty, under a market economy, continue to exist throughout the world bringing hardship to and threatening the lives of hundreds of millions to possibly a few billion people.[6]

Unemployment, underemployment, poverty, unsafe work conditions, unsafe products, destruction of the environment, and other social problems have always been a major result of the market economy for over 200 years, when it got its start in England.[7]

This chapter presents the initial stages of a plan for a development of economic democracy as discussed by Daniel DeLeon.[8] If the market economy is unable to reverse the above social problems, a peacemaking approach to criminology supports the development of such a system. An economic democratic system may very well reverse the above social problems associated with the market economy.

Economic democracy is the shared ownership or domination by the workers of the factories, mills, mines, railroads, land and all other devices of producing. Economic democracy involves the making of goods to satisfy human being requirements, not, as in the market economy, which involves the making of goods for only selling and profit. Economic democracy means true command and management of the industries and social services by the workers through a democratic government based on their economic organization and not controlled and managed by a fraction of a percentage of the population as in the market economy.[9]

Today workers in their respective countries may have the means and the reasons to develop an economy based on democracy and not on profit (as in the market economy). The means include such technology as computers that enable workers to make contact with each other in very short periods of time in order to develop an economic democratic system. The reasons include ending the destruction of our global environment, unsafe work places, unsafe products, unemployment, underemployment, poverty and other social problems. To develop economic democracy, the workers need to prepare on both the political and economic fields.[10]

To develop economic democracy, political agreement under the emblem of a mass political party of labor is needed. The purpose of the party is to teach workers of the need to do away with the market economy, to crusade for the development of class thinking unions, and to declare the power of the working class at the ballot box. The party must also attempt to seize and take apart the political state—the current territorial kind of government—and thus open the process for a different type of government, a cooperating democracy based on industry.[11]

To develop economic democracy, workers also have to join together as a class by organizing new unions. These democratic, rank and file governed unions, made along the programs of industry, while fighting day to day battles for higher pay and a better work environment, are inspired by a bigger goal: supplanting control of the industries and services by a fraction of a percentage of the population with social possession and democratic workers' domination.[12]

While fighting day to day struggles, these unions would strive at directing the whole working class—employed and unemployed, blue collar and white collar—in all occupations. Through an arrangement of elected and retractable representatives, the various unions would be combined by industry and tied together into a big union which would direct a united encounter against the wealthy few who possess and govern the means of producing and apportioning. When the greater number of workers support economic democracy, this big union would back up the determination made at the ballot box by grabbing, maintaining and handling the industries and services of the land in the social interest.[13]

The unions would then advance the governing parts of an economic democratic society. There would be a truly democratic government in which the workers would be in charge of their own economic safety and welfare.[14]

Under economic democracy, all control will start from the workers integrally united in unions. In each workplace, the workers will elect whatever committees or representatives are needed to facilitate production. Within each workplace, the workers will cooperate immediately in conceiving and setting up all strategies essential for effective procedures.[15]

Besides electing all needed workplace representatives, the workers will also elect representatives to a local and national committee of their occupation—and to a central house of representatives representing all occupations. This central House of Representatives will arrange and balance production in all fields of the economy. All people elected to any position in the economic democracy government (the workplace, local committee, national committee or central house of representatives) will be immediately answerable to the workers. They will be subjected to dismissal at any time that a majority of those who elected them determine it is needed.[16]

In conclusion, a development of economic democracy needs great efforts of planning and instructional work. It requires constructing a political party of economic democracy to do away with the market economy and to teach the majority of workers about the necessity for economic democracy. It requires constructing a union uniting all workers in a class-conscious operation and to plan for them to acquire, control and administer the equipment of production.[17]

NOTES

1. David Simon, *Elite Deviance* (Boston: Allyn and Bacon, 1999).

2. Kofi Annan, "Astonishing Facts!" *New York Times*, September 4, 1998, Section 4, p. 16.

3. *Oxfam America,* 1985.

4. Annan, "Astonishing Facts!" 16.

5. Simon, *Elite Deviance.*

6. Socialist Labor Party, *Why America Needs Industrial Democracy* (California: Socialist Labor Party, 2000), and Socialist Labor Party, *The Socialist Programs: What If and How It Developed* (California: Socialist Labor Party, 2000), and Simon, *Elite Deviance.*

7. Socialist Labor Party, *Why America Needs Industrial Democracy, and* Socialist Labor Party. *The Socialist Programs.*

8. Most of this chapter was Louis Gesualdi, "A Development of Economic Democracy" (unpublished paper) originally presented at the Diversity in Research and Society Conference at State University of New York, Farmingdale, NY, April 26, 2001. Also see Daniel DeLeon, *Socialist Reconstruction of Society* (California: New York Labor News, 1977), and Daniel DeLeon, *Socialist Landmarks* (California: New York Labor News, 1952).

9. "The Industrial Democracy of Socialism," *The People*, Vol. 111, no. 3,June 2001, p. 8, Linda Featheringill, "Workers Have to Have a Plan," *The People,* Vol. 106, no. 6, September 1996, "What is Socialism?," *The People,* Vol. 105, no. 6, June 24, 1995, Socialist Labor Party, *Why America Needs Industrial Democracy*, Socialist Labor Party, *The Socialist Programs*, DeLeon, *Socialist Reconstruction of Society,* and DeLeon, *Socialist Landmarks*.

10. Ibid.
11. Ibid.
12. Ibid.
13. Ibid.
14. Ibid.
15. Ibid.
16. Ibid.
17. Ibid.

11

Learning from Leonardo

Walter Issacson in his book *Leonardo Da Vinci* discusses the lessons that we can learn from Leonardo da Vinci in becoming the best creative person that we can be. The more creative individuals that a society has and the more creative a society is, the better that society becomes in science and art. Here is a list provided by Issacson of many of the things that Leonardo da Vinci did during his lifetime. This list below may help us as individuals become the best creative person we can be.[1]

1. Be persistently inquisitive.
2. Pursue knowledge for awareness sake.
3. Notice things.
4. Begin with particulars, specifics, and facts.
5. Respect facts.
6. Reflect visually or pictorially.
7. Understand that art is a science and that science is an art.
8. There are problems we may never solve. Study why.
9. Indulge in the imaginary.
10. Create for yourself not only for other individuals.
11. Work together with other individuals.
12. Construct lists.
13. Write down notes.
14. Be exposed to the unknown.

Individuals may use some of their free time to follow the list above to help in their creative development. Peacemaking criminology encourages individuals to learn the lessons from Leonardo da Vinci in their own creative personal development and using this creativity to help develop a more creative society.

NOTE

1. Walter Issacson, *Leonardo Da Vinci,* New York: Simon and Schuster, 2017.

12

Future Peacemaking Research

Peacemaking Criminology asserts that the excessive concern of American society with street crimes overlooks more serious social problems (such as white collar crimes, corporate crimes, teenage runaways and children being abused at the hands of their relatives).[1] A peacemaking approach to crime and criminal justice affirms that the American public's excessive concern with street crimes leads to unnecessary and unjust laws, harsher punishments that do not work in dealing with crime, and misplaced social resources.[2] Future research by peacemaking criminologists need to provide answers to following the questions and problems that are hidden when American society focuses mainly on street crimes.

- What is the actual amount of crime (including white collar crimes, corporate crimes, teenage runaways and children being abused at the hands of their relatives and their relatives' friends) in America?
- Why is law enforcement in the United States not capable of dealing with crime?
- Is their real fairness and impartiality in our courts?
- What are the vested concerns of the criminal justice activity?
- What spin-off wrongdoings are produced by the drug war?
- How much corruption of government of government officials are outcomes from the criminalization of drugs?
- What ratio of the public want vice-related services and products?
- Is there a mutually beneficial relationship between government and corporate crimes?

- Is there a connection between street crime and white collar crimes?
- Who pays the $250 billion to over a trillion dollars price tag of corporate and white collar crimes?[3]

NOTES

1. See Victor E. Kappeler and Gary W. Potter. *The Mythology of Crime and Criminal Justice,* Long Grove, IL:

Waveland Press, 2018 and see Stephen M. Rosoff, Henry N. Pontell and Robert Tillman, *Profits without Honor*

White-Collar Crime and the Looting of America, Upper Saddle River, NJ: Pearson, 2019. Also, see James William Coleman. *The Criminal Elite: Understanding White-Collar Crime*, New York, NY: Worth Publishers, 20005, see www.zippia .com and see www.financierworldwide.com.

2. Ibid.

3. See Kappeler and Potter. *The Mythology of Crime and Criminal Justice,* 2018.

Bibliography

Abadinsky, Howard. *Organized Crime,* Chicago, IL: Nelson Hall, 1985.

Alfano, M. "Negative Stereotype Persist though FBI Figures Reveal Facts," *ComUnico Magazine,* April 2002.

Americans of Italian Decent: A Study of Public Images, Beliefs and Misperceptions, Washington, D.C.: The National Public Opinion Research Commission for Social Justice Order Sons of Italy, 1991.

Annan, Kofi "Astonishing Facts!" *New York Times,* September 4, 1998.

Arieti, Silvano. *Creativity. The Magic Synthesis.* New York: Basic Books, 1976.

Augustus, John. *John Augustus: First Probation Officer.* New Jersey: Patterson Smith, 1972.

Block, A. and Scarpitti, F. *Poisoning for Profit: The Mafia and Toxic Waste,* New York, NY:

William Morrow, 1985.

B. J. S. Bulletin, *Bureau of Justice Statistics Bulletin, Criminal Victimization,* 1993, 1989.

Braswell, Michael, John Fuller, and Bo Lozoff. *Corrections, Peacemaking and Restorative Justice: Transforming Individuals and Institutions.* Cincinnati, OH: Anderson Publishing Company, 2001.

Bureau of Justice Statistics, U.S. Department of Justice, "Jail Inmates, 1993-1994," April, 1995.

Cauchon, D. "Head of BCCI-Link Bank Quits," *USA Today,* August 15, 1991.

Capozzola, Richard A. *Finalmente: The Truth about Organized Crime,* Altamonte Springs, FL.: Five Centuries Books, 2001.

Chambliss, William. *On the Take: From Petty Crooks to Presidents,* Bloomington: Indiana

University Press, 1978.

Charon, Joel M. *Sociology: A Conceptual Approach.* Boston: Allyn and Bacon, 1989.

Coleman, James W. *The Criminal Elite: Understanding White-Collar Crime.* New York: St. Martin's Press, 2005 and 1998.

Correctional Association of New York, New York, NY, 1998.

Dal Cerro, Bill. *Italian Culture on Film, 1928-1999,* Floral Park, NY: Italic Studies Institute

Image Research Project, 1999.

DeLeon, Daniel. *Socialist Reconstruction of Society.* California: New York Labor News, 1977.

————. *Socialist Landmarks.* California: New York Labor News, 1952.

Elikann, Peter. *The Tough on Crime Myth.* New York: Insight Books, 1996.

Featheringill, Linda, "Workers Have to Have a Plan," *The People,* Vol. 106, no. 6 (September 1996).

Fivecivilizedtribes.org.

Fuller, John R. *Criminal Justice: A Peacemaking Perspective.* Boston: Allyn and Bacon, 1998.

Richard Gambino, "America's Most Tolerated Intolerance: Bigotry against Italian Americans,"

The Italian American Review (Spring/Summer) 1997.

Gesualdi, Louis. "Popularly Held Beliefs about Italian Americans and Organized Crime." *The*

Italian American Experience: A Collection of Writings. Lanham, Maryland: University Press of America, 2012.

————."Peacemaking Acts and Programs to Cut Adult and Teen Crime." *Sociological Viewpoints* 19, (2003): 7-10.

————. "A Development of Economic Democracy." Unpublished paper, presented at the Diversity in Research and Society Conference at State University of New York, Farmingdale, NY, April 26, 2001.

————. "The Work of John Augustus: Peacemaking Criminology." *Academy of Criminal Justice Sciences ACJS Today* 17, no. 3 (1999): 1, 3-4.

————."Popularly Held Beliefs about Italian Americans and Organized Crime" (chapter), co-authored with Francis N. Elmi and Lisa Kuan. *The Italian Americans: A Multicultural View.* New York, NY: Hamilton Books, 2020.

Issacson, Walter. *Leonardo Da Vinci,* New York: Simon and Schuster, 2017.

Italic Institute of America, "Exhibit A: Examples of Media, Bias," italic.org/anti-defamation/Exhibit A. Php, 2015.

Italic Institute of America, "Film Study 2015 (1914-2014)," italic.org/media watch/ film study. Php, 2015.

Kappeler, Victor E. and Potter, Gary W. *The Mythology of Crime and Criminal Justice,* Long

Grove, IL: Waveland Press, 2018

Kappeler, Victor, Mark Blumberg, and Gary Potter. *The Mythology of Crime and Criminal Justice.* Illinois: Waveland Press, 2000 and 1996.

Lichter, S. Robert and Amundon Daniel R. *Portrayal of Italian American Character in Prime*

Television Series, 1994-1995, Washington, D.C.: Social Justice Order Sons of Italy, 1996.

Lujinnos, Carol Chiago "The Only Real Indian is the Stereotyped Indian" in Coramae Richey

Mann and Marjorie S. Zatz (eds.) *Images of Color Images of Crime,* CA: Roxbury Publishing Co., 1998.

Males, Mike. *Framing Youth: Ten Myths about the Next Generation.* Maine: Common Courage, 1999.

———. *The Scapegoat Generation: America's War on Adolescent.* Maine: Common Courage Press, 1996.

Mancuso Janice Therese, "Searching for Italian American History" (paper) presented at the

American Italian Sociohistorical Association First Conference Series entitled *The Italian*

American Experience: A Sociohistorical Examination held at St. John's University, Queens,

NY on October 21, 2015.

Messner, Steven, and Richard Rosenfeld. *Crime and the American Dream.* California: Wadsworth Incorporated, 1994.

Mills, J. *The Underground Empire: Where Crime and Government Embrace,* New York:

Doubleday, 1986.

Morris, Glenn T. "For the Next Seven Generations: Indigenous Americans and Communalism." *Communities Directory.* Langley, Washington: Fellowship for Intentional Community.1995.

Muscogeenation.com

Nadelmann, Ethan. "Drug Prohibition in the United States: Costs, Consequences, and Alternatives." *Science* 245, no. 4921 (1989): 939-947.

Oxfam America, 1985.

Pepinsky, Harold, and Richard Quinney. eds. *Criminology as Peacemaking.* Bloomington: Indiana University Press, 1991.

Rand, Michael R., James P. Lynch, and David Cantor. "Criminal Victimization, 1973-95." *Bureau of Justice of Statistics, National Crime Victimization Survey,* 1997.

Reiman, Jeffrey and Leighton, Paul. *The Rich Get Richer and the Poor Get Prison: Ideology, Class and Criminal Justice,* New York, NY: Routledge, 2023.

Reiman, Jeffrey. *The Rich Get Richer and the Poor Get Prison: Ideology, Class and Criminal Justice.* Boston: Allyn and Bacon, 1998.

Rosoff, Stephen, Henry N. Pontell, and Robert Tillman. *Profit without Honor: White-Collar Crime and the Looting of America.* Upper Saddle River, NJ: Prentice Hall, Incorporated, 2019, 2002 and 1998.

Sex, Drugs and Democracy. Documentary Film, directed by Jonathan Blank. 1994. Netherlands: Red Hat Productions, 2001. DVD.

Shi, Leiyu and Singh, Douglas A. *Essesntials of the U.S. Health Care System.* Burlington, MA:

Jones & Bartlett Learning Books) 2023

Simon, David. *Elite Deviance.* Boston: Allyn and Bacon, 1999.

Simon, David R., and Frank Hagan. *White-Collar Deviance.* Boston: Allyn and Bacon, 1999.

Snyder, Howard N. "Arrests of Youth 1990." *Juvenile Justice Bulletin, U.S. Department of Justice,* January 1992.

Socialist Labor Party. *Why America Needs Industrial Democracy.* California: Socialist Labor Party, 2000.

Socialist Labor Party. *The Socialist Programs: What If and How It Developed.* California: Socialist Labor Party, 2000.

"The Industrial Democracy of Socialism," *The People,* Vol. 111, no. 3 (June 2001).

Trebach, Arnold, and Eddy Engelman. "Why Not Decriminalize?" *New Perspective Quarterly.* Summer (1989): 40-45.

U.S. Bureau of the Census, Washington: Government Printing Office, 1993 and 1970.

Van Ness, Daniel, and Karen H. Strong. *Restoring Justice.* Cincinnati, OH: Anderson, 1997.

Walker, Samuel, Cassie Spohn, and Miriam DeLone. *The Color of Justice: Race, Ethnicity, and Crime in America.* California: Wadsworth Publishing, Company, 1996.

"What is Socialism?" *The People,* Vol. 105, no. 6 (June 24, 1995).

World Data. Info.

www.fincancierworldwide.com.

www.thinkglobalhealth.org.

www.zippia.com.

Yang, Andrew. *The War on Normal People,* New York, NY: Hachette Books, 2018, pages 197-204.

Zogby International, *National Survey: American Teenagers and Stereotyping,* Utica, NY: Zogby International, 2001.

Index

About the Author

Louis Gesualdi is a professor of sociology at the College of Professional Studies, St. John's University. He received his Ph.D. in sociology from Fordham University in 1988. He has published the following books, *The Italian Immigrants in Connecticut, 1880-1940, The Italian/American Experience: A Collection of Writings, A Peacemaking Approach to Criminology: A Collection of Writings, The Bad Things You Have Heard about Italian Americans Are Wrong: Essays on Popular Prejudice,* and *A Source Book of Karl Marx's Letters about Abraham Lincoln and His Strategic Goal in the Civil War: The Destratification of American Society* and coauthored with Francis Elmi and Lisa Kuan *The Italian Americans: A Multicultural View.*